Keep On Walking

Jeana Willis

*Editors Christy Smith
&
Caron Suzanne Davis*

Keep On Walking

Dedication

    First of all, I would like to give honor and glory to my beloved Father God. Without Him I don't even have my breath. I owe my life to Him. He is truly the Love of my life, the reason for my hope. I would not be here today except for the amazing grace and mercy of my Father God.

    I would like to thank my Precious Momma, who was the very first one to teach me of the transforming, all powerful, love of Father God. She taught me the importance of the Word of God, and she led me by example. I am forever thankful to her for never giving up on me, even in the darkest of times.

    Lastly, though certainly not least, I want to give thanks and honor to my beloved husband, Jerry, who saw the gifts Father God had given me even before I knew they were there. He is the one who talked to my publisher about my writing, even before I did.

He has stuck with me through the best and worst of times. He has been with me from the beginning, and at times pushed me when I wanted to give up. I'm so thankful to him for helping me not to just "settle" for ordinary...but to go after and pursue the vision Father God placed in my heart. I feel certain I would not have begun writing if it were not for him. God joined us together, and I am so very thankful for all your love and support.

I pray this book inspires countless others to discover and pursue the gifts Father God has placed inside them to be used for His glory!

"For I know the thoughts that I think toward you, says the Lord, thoughts of peace and not of evil, to give you a future and a hope." (*NKJV*, Jeremiah 29:11). God Bless and KEEP ON WALKING!

Keep On Walking

Copyright © Jeana Willis 2015

All rights reserved. No part of this book may be used or reproduced by any means, graphic, electronic or mechanical, including photocopying, recording or taping or by any information storage retrieval system without the written permission of the publisher except in the case of brief quotations embodied in critical articles and reviews.

Al Scripture taken from the NKJV of the Bible

Whosoever Press books may be ordered through booksellers or by contacting:

Whosoever Press
P.O. Box 1513
Boaz, AL 35957
www.whosoeverpress.com
1-256-706-3315

Because of the dynamic nature of the Internet, any web addresses or links contained in this book may have changed since publication and may no longer be valid. The views expressed in this work are solely those of the author and do not necessarily reflect the views of the publisher, and the publisher hereby disclaims any responsibility for them.

Cover Photo Provided by Cody Stricklin
Copyright © Cody Stricklin

ISBN-13: 978-0692564431 (sc)

Library of Congress Control Number: 2015956121

Printed in the United States of America

Whosoever Press date: 11/1/2015

Table of Contents

Introduction	1
A Sticky Mess	2
All This Noise Inside My Head	5
Can I Just Stay Here?	7
Choices	9
Comparing ... Not Wise	11
Dare To Dream Again!	13
Death No Longer Holds Him	15
Destiny	17
Does It Bother You What People Think of Your Appearance?	20
Don't Just Lose the Weight, Add Something! Build Some Strength	22
Eat the Meat, Throw Away the Bones	25
Enjoy the Blessings, But Don't Neglect the One Who Gave Them	28
Establish My Steps	30
Fear and Worry	32
Feelings Aren't Facts!	33
First One Way, Then Another	36
Friendly Competition	38
Get Into Position!	40
Get Rid of It!	43
Get You Out? Nah, Just Gonna Go In With You!	45
Grace ...Without It, Where Would We Be?	47
He Picked Me Up	48
Healing	50
Heart of Worship	52
Heaven's Eternal Home	54
He's Still Working on Me	56
Hindsight is 20/20	60
His Plans Don't Vary	63
I Just Wanted to Say	65

I May Not Know	67
I Trust You, Father	68
If Need Be	69
I'm Going to Finish!	71
I'm So Glad You Know I'm Human	73
In the Silence	75
In the Sorrow of My Heart	76
Isn't It Grand?	79
It's the Little Things	80
I've Searched for Joy In Lots of Things	82
Jewels	84
Just One Word	85
Keep on Walking, My Faithful Friend	86
Keep Pressing	88
My Dearest Friend	90
My Hope Is In You, Lord	91
No Greater Love	93
Not Yet, Got a Little Pruning to Do!	95
Obedience	96
Oh, Glorious Magnificent Thought	98
On Being Healed	99
One Act of Obedience	101
One Right Decision	103
Only Trust Him	104
Press Through the Pain	106
Qualified	108
Quit Rehearsing!	111
Remember the Lemon Drops!	113
Seemingly Silent	115
Settling in Silence	117
Sometimes I Get Sideways	119
Spectacular Grace	121
Tell Me	122
Thankful	124
That Resurrection Morning	126
The Champion Steps In	127

The Gift Inside	128
The River of God	130
This World Ain't Always Sunshine and Roses	131
Though I May Not Understand How This Can Be Part of Your Plan	133
Tomorrow Is Not Promised	134
Wham!	135
What About Those Spots?	137
What Would You Do?	139
When You Tell Someone	140
Who Makes Me Thankful	141
Why Not Me?	143
You Are Mine	145
You Have a Purpose	147
Author Bio	148

Foreword

I first met Jeana in June of 2012. She and her husband came to our church, and I saw her in the audience a Sunday or two. I introduced myself to her, or maybe she introduced herself to me. I honestly can't quite recall. What I do recall is not long after they came; they were helping out on the stage. Her husband was playing the guitar, and she was behind the microphone. She was so bubbly and full of life. She had some awesome, spikey hair, and an obvious love for Christ. Her excitement for Him, and His Word was evident. She sang like nobody's business and helped to usher our congregation into His presence each Sunday. I knew there was something special about her. She had such a sweet spirit, and it's become more and more evident over the years.

I have been blessed as she has shared with me her struggles, her testimony, and the place from which God has brought her. There are some people who wouldn't want their new Pastor's wife to know so much about their past. Jeana realizes her testimony. Once she started walking on a regular basis, she began to post on Facebook lengthy posts after she went walking. It was always full of truth and insight. One day in particular, I remember messaging her to tell her that what she wrote spoke to me personally that day. This happened right after she started writing or at least right after I realized that's what she was doing. It was something I needed to hear, and I appreciated her allowing God to use her. So many times as a Pastor's wife, you need encouragement. You need to be challenged. You need to be reminded.

As I read these poems, I could see her heart. The emotions are raw. The devotions, thoughts and insights throughout this book, some of them I remember reading on her Facebook wall. I remember her speaking to me about them. In one of her entries called "Get Into Position!" she is such a treasure. See, I remember that day. I remember our walk, I remember us both pushing each other just "one more time around the block." How often, when we need to push ourselves and God sends someone alongside to give us a nudge, or maybe He even does it. Isn't that just how awesome He is?

She and I have become much closer these last three years. I was even blessed to have her move a street over from me! She's now my neighbor. I see her walking each day. On occasion, I'll give her a quick text and ask to join her. A lot of times I don't. Why? Not because I don't love her company, her words of wisdom, but because I know this is her time with the Lord that she so treasures. He speaks to her in some way each and every time she's out there. She's allowing Him to mold her into a new creature each day. She's always so sweet to say "Come on Sista!" She is an inspiration to each and every one she meets.

  I can remember as a new Pastor's wife, I felt inadequate. I often wondered if God knew what He was doing! Ha! I never doubted my husband in his capacity that Christ placed him, but it took me awhile to realize that He chose me to be alongside my husband. I didn't have to be anyone else but myself. Jeana can tell you, I'm not your "normal" pastor's wife, but I'm real. She knows that about me. There are also days I still feel that way. Many times on those days, that's when I can look at Jeana's writings and it uplifts me. It strengthens me. It blesses me. I know that Jeana questioned herself and asked God many times about writing this book, but she allowed God to enlarge her territory. She trusted Him. So many times, we feel inadequate, not "worthy," or even useable. He is greater though, I'm so glad Jeana allowed Him to use her in the most unlikely way she imagined. It makes me realize when I doubt, I just need to "Keep On Walking." Be blessed as you read this book.

Paula Bristow
Pastor's wife of Boaz Church of God
Boaz, AL

Introduction

This book is a result of many trials, many errors and many lessons learned. Many lessons learned the hard way, some have gotten easier, some, I fought with for a long time. It is my prayer that through the telling of some of my journey, the good and the not so good, that it will inspire others to never never, give up; to get as close to the Father as you can, to follow Him with all of your might and become a vessel of honor fit for the Master's purposes.

Father God most assuredly has our best interest in His heart and mind to mold us into the likeness of His image and to use us for His glory. There is no greater purpose than this! No matter who you are; where you came from or where you are right at this moment, you are loved, you are valuable and you have a purpose in Father God's kingdom plan! Whatever you do, keep your hand in the Master's hand and KEEP ON WALKING!

A Sticky Mess

Good morning friends! I'm thankful today I was able to resume my entire walk! It was quite enjoyable. It's a beautiful day! I'm going to share something, and I hope no one finds it offensive. As I was walking today there was a spot on the track, let's just say well a dog had been there! Yes, you can probably guess it, right? Yes, dog poop on the track!

Anyway, I'm a creature of habit I guess, so even though I knew it was there I guess I wasn't paying enough attention. Every time I went around the track and came back around, I kept gravitating towards that side of the track where I've been walking for a long time now. After a couple of times stepping in or nearly stepping in it, I got the idea! Pay attention and force yourself to walk on the other side, Jeana!

I realize that's how it is in life also. Sometimes we are still so accustomed to things the way they are, the way it's always been. Even if it's not good like the dog poop on the track, we still keep walking the same old way. It takes effort to walk and think differently.

Sometimes we settle for less than God's best because it requires extreme effort on our part. Just like it takes effort for me to walk the track and watch out for things that would trip me up or are just downright stinky and gross, it also takes effort for me to keep myself from settling for this same old path I've always taken; to just do what I've always done. Routine and consistency are good unless they become a hindrance and we're not willing to change when God says it's time. What if God wants to take us on a new journey beyond our limited horizons and ideas? What if He wants to take us to a place we've never been before? The Bible says in (*NKJV*, Isaiah 43:19), "Behold I will do a new thing, now it shall spring forth, shall you not know it? I will make a road in the wilderness and rivers in the desert."

I don't know about you, but I want to be right in the center of the perfect plan God has for my life. With that said, it will require some stretching on our part, some changes and some discomfort. I say let's go for it! I want to be all that my Father God destined for me to be! How about you?

Let's get our spiritual, elastic waist band pants out and do some stretching! Let's overindulge at Father God's table and begin to stretch out into our destiny! Come on! With God's help and guidance, well, who knows where we may end up? I know this though, it's going to be greater than we ever imagined! God bless and yes, KEEP ON WALKING!

All This Noise Inside My Head

All this noise inside my head,
Tries to fill my mind with thoughts of dread.
I want to be free from all care and strife,
Yet I cannot escape all the pain of this life.

This temporary home is not always kind,
Its cares, its challenges can trouble our minds.

Yet there is a way to overcome
Given to us by God's only Son
Jesus has paid the price, you see,
For our minds to be cleansed
Our hearts set free.

He wants to give us peace and more
Fill our hearts with hope and joy.
Yet renewing our minds,
Well, that's up to us.
No need to worry, just simply trust,

He will guide us gently on,
And place in our hearts a brand new song.
We can be renewed day by day,
As we read His Word and humbly obey.

Easy no way, yet possible for sure,
With Jesus as our Savior
We can certainly endure.

Not only endure, but have joy overflowing,
We can calm ourselves and have peace in knowing,
All things work together for our good
On HIS promises we can rest assured.

Can I Just Stay Here?

Can I just stay here
In your warm embrace?
Safe in your arms
No greater place.

Far from the chaos
Of the world outside.
In your presence
Is where I long to hide.

This will sound silly
Because I know I shouldn't care,
But Father I don't want
To lose my hair.

They'll stare at me
And wonder why,
Probably even question
Is she gonna die?

But I've been looked at before,
For all kinds of reasons.
At different times,
Different seasons.

Help me Father,
As we journey through.
Help me only,
To keep my eyes on You.

Help me to share your
Magnificent grace.
Each treatment, please help me
To bravely face.

Help me Lord Jesus
As we journey through.
Help me only
To bring glory to you.

Choices

Have you ever begun a solo part and started on the wrong note, sung the WHOLE song that way in front of the whole church? Talk about embarrassing! Yes, this happened to me recently. Life is like that. Sometimes we get it right, and sometimes we don't. This is where we choose to quit, give up in embarrassment or try again. I believe this is where many people fall by the wayside. We try, we fail; we get embarrassed or hurt and sometimes, sadly, we give up.

Think about Peter in the Bible. He actually denied even knowing Jesus three times! What about David? He had an affair, and had the woman's husband killed! I'm sure they were both embarrassed to face the Master again, yet face Him they did; and they were both still greatly used by Father God in spite of their weaknesses, despite of their failings.

There are no perfect people, only our Father God is perfect. One of the most amazing things I have learned in my walk with Father God is this: no matter how embarrassed I am, no matter how bad I mess things up, my Father's love for me, His acceptance of me *does not change*. I have also learned there will be success, and yes, failure. It's what we choose to do with each one that counts. When we succeed, give God the glory. When we fail, if its sin, then repent and accept forgiveness; or if it's simply hitting a wrong note, realize we are just human, we all make mistakes. Get up and try again! Accepting His grace is our choice.

Today, let's choose. Forgetting those things which are behind, and reaching forward to those things which are ahead. "Brethren, I do not count myself to have apprehended; but one thing *I do*, forgetting those things which are behind and reaching forward to those things which are ahead." (*NKJV*, Philippians 3:13).

Comparing ... Not Wise

Ever notice that when you begin to really make progress in a certain area of your life, it's so easy to neglect or just keep the other "little" things in line? Yeah: me too. Being late for work for instance, yes, this is an example from my own life, at times. Ever notice how we humans are quick to point out the areas of our strengths, yet we really don't like to be confronted about the lingering weaknesses in our lives? We all have them.

We humans also like to compare our lives and circumstances at times with those of others. We at times, feel sorry for ourselves and think we have it so much worse than everyone else. While one may be raising children and constantly busy, someone else may suffer from chronic illness that we know nothing about. Many people suffer from a hurt, a devastation that only Father God knows about.

The Bible says in (*NKJV*, 2 Corinthians 10:12), "For we dare not make ourselves of the number, or compare ourselves with those that commend themselves: but they measuring themselves by themselves, and comparing themselves among themselves, are not wise."

At times, we want to feel better about ourselves and maybe we are tempted to compare what we are doing with what someone else may be called to do. The fact of the matter is this, *each one of us*, will give our own account of what Father God has required of us to Father God Himself. We won't be able to point out what someone else did or did not do. We will be held accountable for our own responsibilities. Instead of looking around to see what everyone else is doing, how about we just stay focused on keeping our own "ducks in a row." Life will be so much easier that way. That's really all we can do anyway. KEEP ON WALKING!

Dare to Dream Again!

The words of an old country song came to my mind today, yes an, old country song. You see, Father God can use whomever, whatever, He chooses to speak to us, His children. The words that came to mind were, "Why Not Me?" You may not relate to this, or maybe, just maybe you will. I have had some thoughts, I have not dared to really call them dreams, because then you own them. When you own it, it means that it's a desire of yours, maybe even a plan Father God has for you. What if I'm too scared to see it through? What if people laugh at me? What if I'm just too lazy to put forth the effort it takes to succeed? What about this one, I tried before and it didn't work out, all hell broke loose in my circumstances and in my mind. That's a tough one.

    I was reading about Job in the Bible this morning, about all the devastation he went through, everything he lost. In the end though, it all came out for his good and for God's glory! I can look back at times in my life when I was hurting so badly that I wondered if I'd lose my mind. There were times I thought I just couldn't take it anymore. I felt I could never do what I felt Father God was calling me to do. I tried to just let it go, get on with life and do my own thing, and for a while I did just that. I did what was comfortable for me, until Father God began to awaken the dream inside me again!

You may find yourself in this situation today. You have let fear, insecurity, past failures, hurts and disappointments smother your dream. Today I challenge you, *dare to dream again!* Father God has not changed His mind about you! You see, Father God has a plan. He has not forgotten you. He loves you beyond your wildest dreams! Come on let's dream again, I dare ya! KEEP ON WALKING! (*NKJV*, Jeremiah 29:11).

Death No Longer Holds Him

That dreadful day
When all was quiet
The enemy laughed
He thought he had triumphed

Then three days later
A rumbling was heard
The stone is being rolled back
A miracle has occurred

Jesus has done it
He has risen from the dead
Death no longer holds Him
It is finished like He said

Now Jesus lives forever
Our sin debts paid in full
I'm still astounded by His mercy
My blessed Savior, risen Lord

No chain was strong enough
To keep Him in the grave
He rose to mighty victory
You and I, our lives to save

Do you ever wonder?
If He still loves you after all
My friend, He chose to give His life
Before you even called

Even now, He's calling
Waiting for you to return
Can't you hear Him calling?
My child, won't you please come home?

Destiny

"When my heart is overwhelmed; lead me to the rock that is higher than I." (*NKJV*, Psalm 61:2). I've been having a few issues with my hip and feeling overwhelmed, so I haven't been walking as much the last few days. Have you ever felt that way? We call it 'out of sorts, blue, depressed,' any number of things. While at times, there may be physical reasons for the feelings of despair and depression, with me I find it happens when I really begin to reach out to fulfill my destiny in Christ. As many of you know, my walking has become very important to me, it's an extension of my prayer time, and I just love being outside and hearing God speak to me through whatever is going on around me, not to mention how much better I feel when I walk!

    I absolutely love to hear that someone else has enjoyed or been touched by what Father God gives me to write. My heart's cry is for the Lord to receive glory and honor through my life; to be used by Him to help someone else is the greatest honor I could ever hope for. Have you ever been in a situation like this where you dared to ask Father God for Him to use you and then all hell breaks loose in your mind?

I'm not trying to be overly dramatic it's just the truth, at least for me anyway. Maybe you think I'm telling too much of my business and that I shouldn't be, but I have asked Father God to use me to help others, and I know that I'm not the only one!

I've been here before in some sense and when the pressure pushes: pushes against us, we have two choices. We can retreat and go back to what's comfortable, what does not go against the flow; or where not much is required of us; and do what we feel like doing; just kind of going through the motions and live halfway until we die. Or we can choose to cling to the Master's outstretched hand, and let Him raise us up higher than we ever dreamed possible! God has a plan for each of our lives to prosper and not to harm us, to give us a hope and a future. You see, whether I can walk as many miles today as I want or not, my Father God is faithful to perfect that which concerns me.

He is faithful to remind me that we can do all things through Jesus Christ who strengthens us! We must not depend on our own ability, but cling to the Father God's hand, and trust in His amazing grace. While I was able to physically walk only one mile today, in my spirit I walked many more than that, because my Father God met with me here and spoke to my heart, "It's not about what you can do Jeana, it's all about what I can do in and through you!" God bless and KEEP ON WALKING!

Does It Bother You What People Think of Your Appearance?

Does it bother you what people think of your appearance; your uniqueness; when they make fun of you? Should it? NO! Does it? At times, yes, but others won't. We don't always understand. While yes, we should do our best to be Godly examples, filled with the knowledge that we are to be a light in this world, we don't always get it right.

First, we all sin and fall short of God's glory. This is *everyone*, not just you! At the same time, others won't always approve; accept your gifting. At times, Father God will use others to confirm what He has already shown you.

At other times, the enemy will also try to use others to stop you from doing what Father God has told you in your spirit. You know what He has placed in your heart. Allow Him to develop you; your gifts, so that you will be able to use them for His glory. This "developing process" is extremely difficult at times, but *so necessary*. Gifts without focus and order can also be detrimental to others. We must have that time in the "darkroom" to be developed. Even Jesus went through alone times. It's all part of a grander scheme; a process; but in the end, it's a "refining process!" Father God wants to "shine us up," but *all for His glory* so others can see Him, through us! God bless and KEEP ON WALKING!

Don't Just Lose the Weight, Add Something! Build Some Strength

I am so thankful today for the ability to get out and walk! I was never one to exercise much growing up or in adulthood, and it showed, but Father God has been so faithful to me. He has healed my feet along with the healing from Hepatitis C, and now I am seeing again how much more energy I have and how much better I feel when I walk; the thirty-five pounds gone, and a few sizes smaller. Praise Him!

Today I wanted to share something Father God spoke to my heart while walking. I recently added the 4th mile, along with some weights my friend Ewayne, gave me. In just a few days, I have two more pair of pants I can get into, and I'm burning more calories while walking; also I can tell the difference in my arms.

This got me to thinking. Many times, we may quit eating as much and lose weight. Yet to build muscle, we may need to *add* some weights, some resistance, to kick it up a notch. It's the same thing spiritually. The scripture that came to my mind is, "But also for this very reason, giving all diligence, add to your faith virtue, and to virtue knowledge, to knowledge self-control, to self-control perseverance, to perseverance godliness, to godliness brotherly kindness, and to brotherly kindness love. For, if these things are yours and abound, you will be neither barren nor unfruitful in the knowledge of our Lord, Jesus Christ." (*NKJV*, 2 Peter 1:5-8).

So many times, I believe the reason we don't see more victorious living is because we are trying to simply quit doing some things, without adding some things. Yes, Father God forgives us when we repent. He will help us. He will deliver us. He will strengthen us. Perhaps it's time though, for us to add some weight; build some stamina; fast more; pray more; love others more; and use our spiritual muscle. Perhaps the reason we are going through a particular trial is Father God simply adding some weight, causing us to develop strength and muscle we never knew we had!

It's not enough to just lay down the old life. We must learn to live the new one! I'm so astounded at how Father God takes a simple physical illustration to speak to my heart.

Today, has He called you to lay aside something; maybe a sin, or maybe just a distraction? Rest assured He has something far better for you in mind. It may seem heavy at first, and like a burden at times. If Father God has called you to carry it, rest assured, you're building spiritual muscle, to be able to stand against the attacks of the enemy and maybe help someone else along their journey as well; and that my friend is something far more valuable than any physical strength! God bless and KEEP ON WALKING!

Eat the Meat, Throw Away the Bones

Lately, I've been thinking about how to adjust my schedule so that I can fit into it everything I need to get done. My walking time is very important to me for more than one reason; yet I am going to have to adjust it. You may say, "Who cares about your walking schedule, lady?" Hold on, maybe you'll connect with what I'm about to say, or maybe not. Eat the meat. Throw away the bones!

I love my early morning walks at the park. I hear Father God speak to me a lot of times as I am just walking, praying, and enjoying His beautiful creation; not to mention the weight, and inches lost benefit also.

I've been thinking though, there are some specific areas I am going to have to target if I want to see them change. The walking is great, yet it hit me, I may need to add some floor exercises, etc. to get to those stubborn places that are not wanting to move!

The same is true spiritually. Yes, we are saved by Father God's amazing grace.

We are saved, but are we walking in full freedom? There may be some things we will need to lay aside, trim some things back, in order to make room for what Father God, is wanting to do in our lives. We may have to let some things go to make more time for Father God and His Word, to give Him first priority in our lives.

Our walk with Father God is a daily thing. There are spiritual exercises we must do, if we want to stay in shape spiritually. We cannot be healthy if we are only "eating" twice a week at church. We must discipline ourselves, and feed daily on the Word of Father God. We may be doing exceptionally well in some areas, yet refusing to work (exercise) the other ones. It is usually the ones we are experiencing victory in that we like to talk about; not so much about the ones we are lacking.

I know for me, Father God has shown me specifically some areas I need to concentrate on and change. Father God wants His children blessed and free. Blessing though, comes from obedience. As we work on the outer man, let's not forget to exercise the spiritual man also. There is a scripture that says, "But let patience have its perfect work, that you may be perfect and complete, lacking nothing." (*NKJV*, James 1:4). KEEP ON WALKING!

Enjoy the Blessings, But Don't Neglect the One Who Gave Them

Many times, we pray for things, even good things. We are blessed with them, and we get so busy taking care of all these "things" that we get our priorities out of proper order.

It may even be something we know God has called us to do. It could be our ministry, or even our friends and family. Of course, these are wonderful blessings from our Lord. Yet, they are never to take His place. We have to carve out time for just the two of us (God and us), and we all know time is a precious commodity.

We can get so busy that we don't spend enough time with our precious Lord. He is the only reason we are supposed to be doing what we're doing.

Our call as Christians is to know Him and to make Him known; and to share His saving grace with others.

If we aren't continually spending time with our Lord, letting *Him* speak to *us*, letting Him restore us and refresh us, we soon run out of energy.

The good news is we have the choice. It will require sacrifice on our part, but we can choose to lay aside something else to make room for time with our Lord. If we don't choose to make time, it won't happen. My prayer is that we will enjoy the blessings our Lord gives. Never let the blessings take time away from the One who blessed us, our precious Lord.

"But seek first the kingdom of God and His righteousness, and all these things shall be added to you." (*NKJV*, Matthew 6:33). God Bless and KEEP ON WALKING!

Establish My Steps

Almost as soon as my feet hit the track this morning, I heard Father God speak to my heart. I so love when this happens! The leaves were completely covering the track in a lot of places so, if you hadn't walked this path before you might not know where exactly to walk. Because I have walked this path for a period of time now, I knew where to place my feet. I kept on walking. That's when it hit me, because I have been walking with my Savior for some time now, I know where to place my trust.

At times, when I can't clearly see, the path ahead of me, and I can't see that curve up ahead. I know that my Father God is orchestrating my path. You see, the Bible says in (*NKJV*, Psalm 40:2), "He also brought me up out of a horrible pit, out of the miry clay, and set my feet upon a rock, *and* established my steps." At times, I may not clearly see the path, yet I can fully trust the One who placed me on this path. I can fully rely on Him to direct and establish my steps.

If you're like me, maybe Father God is doing something new in your life; something that you never dreamed of. Let's just stick to the path we know, and when He chooses to change our direction and lead us on a new journey, well, let's just follow our Leader! He is the Master navigator; He never gets lost. Do you want to know something else? There is no chance He will ever lead us wrong! KEEP ON WALKING!

Fear and Worry

Fear and worry
I cast you down.
You're not welcome here
I don't want you around.

My mind is renewed
By the Word of God.
I'm no longer listening
To the lies you've got.

I'm a daughter of the King
Father God, yes it's true.
I'm created to worship Him
And this I'll do.

I've decided to follow
His plan for my life.
I'm leaving behind all fear and strife

I'm moving forward in His grace, you see,
I'm pressing on ... Wherever He leads.

Feelings Aren't Facts!

Ever notice when you begin to make progress in a certain area, maybe you begin to dream the impossible, and you are immediately met with fear, and uneasiness or confusion? Yes, me too. This is not unusual. The Bible says in (*NKJV*, 1 Peter 4:12), "Beloved, do not think it strange concerning the fiery trial which is to try you, as though some strange thing happened to you;" The thing that's important is that we don't let these "things", these "feelings" stop us! Father God has told us in (*NKJV*, 1 Peter 5:8), "Be sober, be vigilant; because your adversary the devil walks about like a roaring lion, seeking whom he may devour." Take notice of the words here: *"like a roaring lion."* His roar, yes, can be deafening. This is one reason we must choose not to listen to it. He will come and try to scare us with his threats; his roaring, through sickness, financial difficulties, heartache and exhaustion.

The Bible says clearly though, he is no match for Jesus Christ, who lives inside every Christian. You see, he can only devour us if we let him! The Almighty Father God lives in us as believers. There is no way the enemy can defeat us, as long as we cling tightly to the Master's hand, and simply follow Him. (*NKJV*, Isaiah 54:17), says, "No weapon formed against you shall prosper, and every tongue *which* rises, against you in judgment you shall condemn." These aren't my words, they're from our Father!

The reason the devil is fighting you is because *he knows*, rest assured *he knows* when we fully realize *how much* Father God loves us, and that we really can do *all* things through Christ who strengthens us. He does not stand a chance! He will no longer be able to keep us in prison within ourselves, never able to help someone else. This is the reason he fights us so hard. He knows there are giftings placed inside each one of us to be used for the Master, Father God, to help others and to bring glory unto, Himself. We have that choice given to us by Father God Himself! We can continue to live a life of starts and stops, never fully becoming all that Father God created us to be; or we can simply throw ourselves into the arms of the Master; let go of everything that would hinder us going after the dream He has placed inside of us, and begin to walk toward the dream. Every journey begins with a single step, and then another, and another.

Today I chose to simply trust in Father God, put one foot in front of the other, and KEEP ON WALKING! Won't you join me today?

First One Way, Then Another

This morning I have a couple of thoughts I'd like to share. The other day I talked about the leaves covering the track, and being sure where you placed your feet (your trust). I spoke about Father God being faithful to keep us on the right track as long as we follow Him. On a different day, I talked about the leaves representing things that need to be cleaned up in our lives. I spoke of priorities. Isn't it strange, yet wonderful at the same time, how the same situations can speak to us in different ways at different times, and have a totally new meaning!

The Bible says in (*NKJV*, Job 33:14), "For God may speak one way, or in another." That's when the thought hit me; it's just like with the leaves. Father God can use the same situation to teach us more than one thing, if our hearts are open to receive from Him, or whomever/whatever He uses to speak to us. There are some particular times and people in my life that come to mind. I just felt as if I couldn't take anymore! As time passes, I am beginning to see that Father God placed each one of them in my life for a specific reason and season. Every situation can be a learning experience, if we so choose.

Some of the most painful, aggravating and exhausting things in my life were actually tools in my Father's hands to mold me into the woman He desires for me to be. I sure didn't see it then! That's where our faith comes in. This dream He's awakening inside me, well, I guess it's been there all along. I just had to go through some life to uncover it. I am pretty confident, though, it's going to be worth it all.

Many times, we won't understand, but we simply choose to trust Him. This is what I have chosen, to give Father God, my heart; and let Him speak to me and through me. Now I know, all this other stuff is just part of the journey. Father God will use it for our good, His glory, and the good of others if we will just make this one decision; well, maybe two, to simply *trust and obey*. KEEP ON WALKING!

Friendly Competition

While walking this morning, I guess I wasn't walking as fast as usual and a fellow walker passed me. Later on, I noticed him or someone else gaining on me, so I said to myself, "Oh no, you're not passing me!" So, I sped up!

When I first started walking, I can remember being so excited when I could actually pass the people that had been passing me! I know this may sound silly, but actually we, or rather I, have been known to do this even when it comes to other things.

We look at what someone else is doing, and we think we should be doing the same thing, so we end up trying to do what they are doing; yes, even competing at times! Friendly competition is okay I guess, at times, but when it comes to the race of life, the life Father God has given you it's not a competition with others! You are only supposed to run *your* race, to receive the prize God has for you!

You are a unique, one of a kind original! The Bible says in (*NKJV*, 2 Corinthians 10:12), that it is not wise to compare ourselves with others. The scripture says, "For we dare not class ourselves or compare ourselves with those who commend themselves. But they, measuring themselves by themselves, and comparing themselves among themselves, are not wise." The only race you are called to run is your own. Let's not try to do what God has told someone else to do. Let's just get busy running our own race; doing what God has told us to do. He has a plan for you, you know, a plan for each individual person. (*NKJV*, Jeremiah 29:11), says, "For I know the thoughts that I think toward you, says the Lord, thoughts of peace and not of evil, to give you a future and a hope." God bless and yes, KEEP ON WALKING!

Get Into Position!

Wow! What an awesome day; nice day for a walk. Don't you think? I took my walk a little later than usual today. I struggled a little today to get those three miles, but get them I did! I noticed something while I was walking today, and of course, this led to another thought that Father God spoke to my heart, that I felt led to share with you.

I noticed as I was walking today that I was walking with my head down, as if willing myself forward. It seemed almost as if I was literally dragging my limbs behind. This is definitely not the proper posture for walking, especially for long walks! I was wearing myself out!

Proper posture would be head held up, guiding the way, looking forward to a place in the distance, (this helps me with momentum); arms moving, doing their part, (this really helps me with speed); feet making the full step, not walking on the toes! Every part of the body has to do its proper part for my walk to be successful, and be able to finish well, without injury, or simply giving up! I then got to thinking about leadership, whether it is, in our church, our home, or our workplace.

What if only a few people are doing their part; fulfilling their function in the home, the church, at work, etc. It becomes extremely hard to function properly. It's harder on everyone else. We all suffer.

There is a proper order or structure to every one of these places. Each one of us has a specific spot, or role to fill. When we don't, the whole body suffers. If even one part is out of line, just like if our spine is out of line, the rest of our body feels it, and it can be extremely painful.

The Bible says in (*NKJV*, Ephesians 4:15-16), "but, speaking the truth in love, may grow up in all things into Him who is the head—Christ—from whom the whole body, joined and knit together by what every joint supplies, according to the effective working by which every part does its share, causes growth of the body for the edifying of itself in love."

No matter if we are a leader or a lay person; a boss or employee; a husband or wife; a parent or child, we each have a specific role to fill. When we are not in our proper role, it causes the rest of the body, family, workers, etc. to have to work that much harder to take up the slack; and it will leave us unfulfilled because no one can truly fill our call, our part, but us. I struggled a little with my walk today, but I got myself in the right position and was able to accomplish what I set out to do, and even got some encouragement from my sweet friend, my pastor's wife, sister, Paula, along the way! In a nutshell, Father God spoke to my heart again about the importance of each individual, and each individual's purpose.

We are all called to work together; to fulfill a specific purpose, and when we do that everyone benefits. When we don't, there is something lacking, and everyone feels it, whether we recognize it or not.

Today, I encourage you ask Father God, "What is it that you want me to do? Who can I encourage today?" When we are faithful to give whatever encouragement, time, money, talent, meals, etc., that we have, Father God is surely faithful to give us back in abundance, press down, shaken together, and running over! Try Him and see! God bless and KEEP ON WALKING!

Get Rid of It!

It was a little chilly as I went out to walk this morning, so I grabbed a little jacket and began. It is such a beautiful morning! I noticed something as I began to get faster and get a few laps in, I didn't need the jacket anymore! I took it off, tied it around my waist and resumed my walk.
    It wasn't long before I noticed. I felt I was slowing down and that it was harder to keep my pace up because that jacket was tied around my waist. This led to my next thought. *I wonder how many things we let hinder us in our walk with Father God. How many little habits, distractions, insecurities or even sins, do we let hinder us in our walk with Him?*
    What things are we allowing to slow us down? The Bible tells us in (*NKJV*, Hebrews 12:1), "Therefore we also, since we are surrounded by so great a cloud of witnesses, let us lay aside every weight, and the sin which so easily ensnares us, and let us run with endurance the race that is set before us."

Two things catch my attention in this verse. The first one is that *we* must lay aside the weight, the things that are slowing us down.

We must *choose* to get rid of them! They don't just go away on their own. The other is that each of us, as an individual, has a specific race marked out for US! We must run our race, not someone else's.

Father God has created each one of us with strengths, and gifts, that are unique. We also, as humans have weaknesses. What may be a hindrance to one person may not be to another. What might tempt one person may not tempt another. We must pay attention to those things; just like that jacket this morning, if it's hindering us from becoming closer to Father God ... *get rid of it*!

Someone may just be waiting on the gift you have inside of you; someone needs encouraging today; someone needs to know they are loved and cherished by Father God. Let's get rid of all the things that keep us bogged down. We've got work to do! God bless and KEEP ON WALKING!

Get You Out? Nah, Just Gonna Go In With You!

How will we know that He is the fourth man in the fire, if we never go through the fire? How will we know our Father God can deliver us out of (or through) difficult times if we never walk through them?

We are overcomers because we have had something to overcome! His strength is made perfect in our weakness; not in the lack of troubles and hard times; right smack dab in the middle of them; makes me want to shout right there!

Many times, we act as if we are going through these things alone when the exact opposite is true!

(*NKJV*, Daniel 3:25), says, "Look!" he answered, "I see four men loose, walking in the midst of the fire; and they are not hurt, and the form of the fourth is like the Son of God." Don't you remember that He is right there walking through the fire with you? You know what else? The Bible says when they finally came out, they didn't even smell like smoke! Wow!

Now, I think we can walk a little while longer, don't you? After all, we've got the best escort there is, Jesus Christ Himself! KEEP ON WALKING!

Grace ... Without It, Where Would We Be?

Grace ... Without it, where would we be?
Grace ... Amazing, for you and for me.
From the darkness of sin,
He lifted me out
Clothed in His righteousness
Now we can shout.

Because of His sacrifice
We can be free
The price has been paid
By Jesus, our King.

He Picked Me Up

I am sitting here at the park with the most amazing feeling. God, the only true, living God, picked me! I don't say that pridefully, because I know where I came from. I also know what it's like not to be chosen. Do you remember when we were in school in P.E. class, and they would pick two team captains (usually the pretty/handsome, popular kids) and they would pick teams? There were always those last two people that didn't get picked; so they were just put on whichever team's turn it was to get a player. I remember, I was usually one of those last two that weren't chosen.

You may have never felt such embarrassment; such humiliation; such shame. Do I sound overly dramatic? It *is* dramatic as a child to be left out; not wanted or picked for the team, for whatever reason. All a child really understands is that they weren't picked. Shame can be a crippling thing. The enemy comes when we are very young to try to stop us from fulfilling the call Father God has on our lives. He starts very early trying to kill, steal and destroy. He starts with situations just like these. He says things like, "You're not good enough; pretty enough; smart enough;" the list goes on and on.

My journey over the last few years has been extremely difficult at times, yet so necessary. I needed to deal with some past hurts; issues that I was still carrying from a long time ago. I needed to be healed, and I needed to forgive.

I can see now that Father God has used these circumstances to work some stuff out in me, to prepare me for my destiny. Father God, Lord of all, chose me! Wow! This is an amazing revelation, to know that God Almighty *chose us*, not because of anything that we could have ever done; simply because He wanted us on His team! Father God wants a relationship with us!

I am no longer that embarrassed, hurt, shamed little girl that didn't get picked. I am a daughter of the Most High, Father God! I am a princess! You know what? Father God wants *you* on His team as well. All you have to do accept the invitation. Come on, what are you waiting for? There is room for everyone on Father God's team! KEEP ON WALKING!

Healing

Today I wanted to take a moment to explain why I talk so much about my walks. For about two years or so, I could barely stand all day at work, much less go walking. I had been diagnosed with neuropathy, plantar fasciitis and heel spurs. The pain was almost unbearable at times. I went through a series of three shots in each foot, took prescription medication, all the while praying for healing. A change in medicine led to some really bad side effects.

One day, Father God spoke to me. He told me this was not the direction I needed to be going. I flushed them that day and decided that this was simply between me and my Father God! I decided that day that I would deal with the pain if I had to but no more of that medicine. I'm not saying for anyone else to get rid of their medicine. Let's make that clear. This is just what God led me to do. To make a long story short, there was a particular day at church when my pastor at that time, prayed with me for my healing. The date was March 11th, 2012.

Prayer, along with some other direction Father God had given me led to healing in my feet! Now I am able to walk again, three miles a day! Praise Father God! So you see, the reason I'm so excited is not just that I'm losing weight, and not just because I hear the Lord speak to me during my walks; though that *is* my favorite part. It's also not just that I have so much more energy, it's because Father God has healed my feet and put me on a path to freedom and I told him if He did heal me I would surely tell it! Praise Him! KEEP ON WALKING!

Out of My Comfort Zone

While walking this morning, I started singing an old song that refers to giving God more than mere words, and more than what's normal or comfortable. Then the tears just started flowing. I have sung in church for several years, even as a child and it is usually comfortable for me. I love it! There is that feeling when it all comes together and people are all worshiping God together. There's nothing like it. Yet when I got to this line, about giving God my whole heart, I broke down.

Maybe what we think is our only gift is just one of many. Maybe we have other gifts that we have not really dared to pursue because of fear, or maybe the cost of pursuing it. I just know that God requires more than what is comfortable sometimes. I also know that He gives me way more than I deserve. Will I just give Him what is comfortable for me? Will I surrender to the things He is bringing me? Today I say, "Yes Lord, to your plans, yes Lord, to your will."
What about you? What will you bring to the Master today? Will it be *your, very best*? He

deserves it, you know. By the way, today I added the third mile! Who knows what's in store? God bless and KEEP WALKING!

Heaven's Eternal Home

Will the storms come?
Yes, they will,
Sometimes the road you travel
Seems all uphill.

Sometimes the winds are fast and fierce
Sometimes your faith may seem to diminish
But look to the skies where your help comes from,
Our Savior is coming, Jesus Christ, God's Son.

Just in time, He'll come to your rescue,
When you thought it was finished
He says, I'm not through.

It's not over my child
I've seen your faith.
Come with me now,
I've prepared the place.

A place of rest and perfect peace,
Where all pain and suffering cease.
A place of joy like you've never known,
We'll spend forever in heaven's eternal home.

He's Still Working On Me

Many times, we go through seasons in our lives that we don't totally understand, if we understand them at all. Yet, the Bible says that, "The steps of a righteous man or woman are ordered by the Lord." (*NKJV*, Psalm 37:23). I have most certainly found this to be true in my own life. Many times, we don't see how it is that the steps we have to take can, *in any way*, be ordered by Father God. Many times, we may say, "How can this situation ever be for my good?"

Many times, we are placed in situations that can either bring out the best in us, or the worst in us. If the situation brings out the best in us and we are able to respond in the right way with humility, grace and a thankful heart, Praise Father God!

On the other hand, certain situations occur and maybe we just don't handle them very well. We lose our temper, maybe we say something we shouldn't, maybe we gossip, or maybe we react in a way that isn't pleasing to our Father God. You know what? I believe these steps are also ordered by Father God.

Now don't get me wrong. Of course, He doesn't want us to sin and act inappropriately. Yet, He does want us to see our own heart. He wants us to see how far we have come in Him. He also wants us to keep moving forward, growing in His grace, making spiritual progress. He wants us to see those things that still need to change in order to be pleasing to Him. He is faithful to show us those areas we still need to surrender to Him, those sins for which we need to repent, areas in our lives that need correction. That, my friend, is great news!

You may say, how can God showing me my sin, my wrongdoing, be good news? It is simply this. The Bible says in (*NKJV*, Proverbs 3:12), "For whom the Lord loves He corrects, Just as a father the son *in whom* he delights". It's because He loves us that he correct us!

Does this discipline feel good? No, not usually! Especially when it's happening for sure! The Bible says this also in (*NKJV*, Hebrews 12:11), saying that, "Now chastening (discipline) seems to be joyful for the present, but painful. Never the less, afterward it yields the peaceable fruit of righteousness to those who have been trained by it."

We see here that it's because Father God loves us that He corrects us. He also knows exactly what He has planned for our future. He knows just exactly what He is preparing us for! These last two years He has most certainly been showing me some things! Did some of them hurt? You bet they did! As a matter of fact, I'm still working on some things now, as we all will be until He takes us home!

I'm so glad though, that Father God loves us enough to continue to mold and cleanse us, to create in us a clean heart that He can use for His purpose, for His glory! There are many things that just aren't beneficial for this next phase in our journey with Father God. They may not be sin, just time consuming and unnecessary, taking us away from what He has destined for us to do. We have to decide to lay down what's not necessary so that we can do Father God's will.

This will not always be popular or understood. Your life, your gifts, even your ministry may not look the same as everyone else's, and that's okay, as long as you are obeying Father God. Even those closest to you may not always understand. Father God has a specific plan for your life. He says so in (*NKJV*, Jeremiah 29:11).

Little did I realize about 4 years ago, that many of the things Father God was teaching me, He would bless me to be able to share in my upcoming book (something I never dreamed of, until He spoke it to my heart.) KEEP ON WALKING.

Hindsight Is 20/20

I know you've probably all heard the saying, 'hindsight is 20/20.' I find the older I get, the more of life I live, just how true this statement really is. Many times we don't fully realize what is happening as we go through various trials and issues of life, but Father God is teaching us many, many, valuable lessons that can sometimes only be learned through experiences both good and bad.

I have a CD that I have listened to so many times I can quote portions of it! The minister asked the question, "What do you do when you've done all you know how to do and still the situation remains the same?" What do you do when God lets you cry yourself to sleep at night? What do you do when He doesn't explain why? What do you do when He doesn't take away the pain but allows you to bear it? I have found the only way to make it through these times is to, by faith, cling even more tightly to Father God and His word!

I have found the only constant, the only true source of everlasting comfort and hope is in Father God and His Word. Whatever season we find ourselves in, no matter what pain or discomfort we may see, we must cling to the One who gives us our very breath! Though He may not seem to be answering, we must cling more tightly to Him even when we don't understand.

Father God is much more interested in our growth than in our comfort. He knows exactly what circumstances will work out for our good, to ultimately bring us closer to Him and to bring Him glory. The Bible says in (*NKJV*, 1 Peter 1:6-7), "In this you greatly rejoice, though now for a little while, *if need be*, you have been grieved by various trials, that the genuineness of your faith, being much more precious than gold that perishes, though it is tested by fire, may be found to praise, honor, and glory at the revelation of Jesus Christ." There must be a need, if He is allowing us to go through something!

Though we may not understand it at the time, Father God is always working things out for our good! I guarantee. God doesn't lie! When He tells us, that on the other side of this season, we will be able to look back and say, "My Father God is faithful!" He always has been, and He always will be! God bless and KEEP ON WALKING!

His Plans Don't Vary

His plans don't vary,
They don't change.
Even when our lives,
We try to arrange.

What He planned in the beginning
He still will do.
My friend, He's only
Waiting on you.

Why do we run
And try to escape?
For it's only a masterpiece
He wants to create.

Broken dreams
Unfulfilled plans
Come back to life
In the Father's hands.

He will take the remnants
Of your broken heart,
Put them together
And give you a new start.

Keep On Walking

Hope and healing
Are waiting on you
He will give you the courage
To see you through.

If you'll only quit trying
To escape His plan.
Rest in His love
Surrender to His plan.

There you'll find rest
For your weary soul.
There you'll find comfort
And be made whole.

I Just Wanted To Say

I just wanted to say a quick good morning and encourage you to *never give up!* I have been really busy these last couple of days and haven't had time to share with you. I have been so tired! While I was walking this morning, I realized I only had time for about two miles instead of my usual three. I had other errands to run, so I couldn't fit everything into my neat little schedule the way I wanted. Don't you hate when that happens?

That's when Father God spoke to my heart and said, "You don't have to do everything perfectly. You simply do what you can, the best you can, and that's all I require." Isn't this wonderful news? All that Father God requires is that we do our best, not our best compared to someone else, just *our* best!

We must never let fear of not doing everything perfectly keep us from even trying! Anyone can quit. It doesn't take much strength for that. The person who succeeds is the one that puts their trust in Father God, does the best they can, and when they mess

up, they simply get back up and try again!
KEEP ON WALKING!

I May Not Know

I may not know the "proper" thing
I guess I'm not considered "cool"."
Still as HE leads me, I will follow
For it's Him I want to approve.

I'm not looking for everyone to applaud,
Not for fame, or fortune or to travel abroad.
Though these things are splendid, I guess
I simply still long, for My Savior to bless.

It's His heart I'm after
Though really, it's already mine.
It's my heart that's torn and unfaithful at times.

Yet, He's faithful to speak to me
In the center of my soul.
It's Me you're yearning for
Come to Me and be made whole.

I Trust You Father

I trust you Father.
Please help me stand,
Amidst uncertain times at hand.

My flesh is weak and crying out,
My heart is breaking as I shout.
Please help my spirit to receive,
Peace and rest, Your blessed reprieve.

I'm simply overwhelmed, it's true,
But even now, I still trust You.
I know You understand my pain,
My fear, my sadness, my heart's refrain.

I know our times are in Your hands.
In Your strength Lord, help me stand.
All glory to You Lord, to You alone.
As I wait before your throne.

For clear direction
I know You will give,
As my life for You I live.

I trust You Father, You alone
Not my will, but Yours be done.

If Need Be

"Wherein you greatly rejoice, though now for a season, if need be, you are in heaviness through manifold temptations." (*NKJV*, 1 Peter 1:6 paraphrased). Sometimes Father God allows us to go through extremely difficult situations so that we can see things about ourselves. Then He gives us the ability to change, or maybe He just wants to prove Himself strong on our behalf!

If He, as our Father, allows us to go through a difficult season, it may well have been a *"need be"* season. Some of us are strong-willed children, and we don't listen the easy way! Other times, we may never know on this side of eternity why we went through a season of great pain and trial.

(*NKJV*, Deuteronomy 29:29), says, "The secret things belong to the Lord." This I do know, that Father God is, always has been, and forever will be faithful to His children. Whatever season of life we find ourselves in, *no season is ever wasted* when we surrender it to Father God!

Don't give up! (*NKJV*, John 10:10), says that "He came that we might have life and life more abundantly!" Come on, we have Almighty God as our Father. Let's go through these seasons and come out on the other side *Victorious*! KEEP ON WALKING!

I'm Going to Finish!

I am so thankful that I was able to walk today. Yesterday was a real struggle. My knee, the one I hurt a few years ago, was giving me fits. I had walked a couple of miles then decided to stop because I was hurting pretty bad, and I didn't want to do any further damage. I had actually gotten in the car and started to leave, then I guess the fighter in me came out and I said, "Oh no, I am going to finish!" I messaged my hubby and told him I was able to finish my whole walk, that yes, I was limping some, but I did finish!

A little bit later, I get a message back. My hubby reminded me of Paul in the Bible. He was shipwrecked, bitten by a snake, and yes, you guessed it, he finished, and finished strong! I said all that to get to this point. You may have been hurt, abused, disappointed with how your life has turned out. You may feel like giving up. You may be in so much pain, spiritually and physically that you don't think things can ever change because of "your limp."

It's not true my sister, my brother! If you will reach out to Jesus Christ, He will help you. He'll hold you up, even if He has to carry you across the finish line. Father God guarantees you will be able to finish and finish strong!

(*NKJV*, Psalm 27:14 paraphrased), says, "Wait on the Lord. Be of good courage and He shall strengthen your heart." Even if you are limping today, don't give up! Father God is faithful; pick your head up! You can do this! KEEP ON WALKING!

I'm So Glad You Know I'm Human

I'm so glad you know I'm human
At times, my flesh is weak.
It strives against my spirit
Only pleasure, it wants to seek.

I'm so glad that you're my Father
That nothing is too hard for You.
I'm so glad to know You hold my hand
While this world I travel through.

I'm glad to know I'm protected
Covered by Your Blood
Cleansed, healed and forgiven
Set apart for Your cause.

Teach me, dear Father
As Your plan unfolds,
To help strengthen the weary
Help lighten their load.

Not to get sidetracked
With my own grand dreams
But to lay them all
At Your dear feet.

Your plan is perfect
Of this I am sure.
Lead me, dear Savior,
As I journey forward.

In the Silence

In the silence, I hear His voice
When I step away from all the noise.
In the quiet He speaks to me,
And molds me into
Who He wants me to be.

I treasure these times
Alone with my Father.
It's in this molding process
I become like the potter.

This is where He gets rid of
the things that do hinder.
And turns this lump of clay
Into a thing of splendor.

Handcrafted by the Master
The Almighty Son of God.
In the silence, I am waiting
For the cleansing, healing touch of God.

In the Sorrow of My Heart

In the sorrow of my heart,
Where justice meets the sinful dark,
I'm overwhelmed with sin and shame.
It's said and done
I'm to blame.

Oh, that I could escape
Its dreadful grip.
But, try as I might
My feet still slip.

I long God's mercy to receive,
But, all my fears cause my heart to grieve.
Oh, that I could escape
This awful place,
And once again
Feel God's warm embrace.

I know His mercy still holds true
And yet, I wonder
Is it for you?
Or have I gone too far this time
What will it take,
This hill to climb?

And then my Father
Draws me near.
You've not gone too far
My child, I'm here.

I've never left
It's you who wandered
From the path
I placed you on
It's in My will
You'll once again be strong.

But for now
Repent and return,
And cling to the lessons
You've painfully learned.

No pain is wasted
No tear unnoticed
When once again
You regain your focus.

To be an obedient
Child of God
Sometimes the path
It's extremely hard.

Yet with each piece of me
That falls away
Father draws me to
A brighter day.

To a love, none greater known
The love of my Father
There's peace and rest
In Him alone.

Isn't It Grand?

Isn't it grand, Divine indeed
That the King of all glory
Would choose you and me?

Isn't it magnificent that He calls us His own?
That boldly we can come before God's throne.

Without fear, we can approach our Father
Because we are His sons and daughters.

Made in His image
Filled with His love,
Cleansed and forgiven
Because of Jesus' shed blood.

He bought us back from the enemy,
When Jesus chose to die on that tree.
No one forced Him
He laid down His life,
He was willing to pay the supreme sacrifice.

Pay it He did, once for all,
Will you today answer His call?

It's the Little Things

Today I've been thinking about these writings of mine. They are quite simple, nothing really profound. They are very easy to understand, some people may even find them silly at times. They are just ordinary, everyday life situations. I have found many days these are the very things we get tripped up over, the things we *think* we can handle on our own. We've got this, right? Maybe not.

We sometimes let the small things build up. We don't want to *bother* Father God with such details. He's got enough to do, right? We try to handle things on our own. We should be strong enough for that. We've got this, we say.

The next thing we know, we've let several small things add up to an overwhelming list of problems and now we're in panic mode!

We all know nothing is too big or too difficult for God to handle. Well, *nothing is too small either*! We like to be self-sufficient, thinking we can take care of ourselves. The truth is we don't even have our breath unless the Lord gives it to us! (*NKJV*, Matthew 10:30), says, "But the very hairs of your head are all numbered."

This lets me know that my Father God pays very close attention to even the smallest of details. You know what else is amazing? Nothing, *absolutely nothing*, is gonna shock Him or make Him change His mind about us. Isn't that just simply amazing? Yes, it is! It most certainly is! KEEP ON WALKING!

I've Searched For Joy In Lots of Things

I've searched for joy in lots of things
For peace and hope and happiness
I've longed to find what life's all about
My one true purpose, what will make my life count.

It's not in money, houses or lands
Though I guess to have them would be quite grand.
It's not in pleasures that this world can afford,
True joy I've found in Jesus my Lord.

True joy is knowing that my name is written
In the Lamb's Book of Life.
That I have been forgiven.

Knowing one day
Jesus will come again for me,
And forever I'll be with Him
And together we will spend eternity.

In that land that God has promised
Never a tear shall fall.
I hope that you will join me
Won't you accept the Savior's call?

The Father now is waiting
To heal your very soul.
Why not come to Him today?
Be cleansed and be made whole.

Jewels

You don't realize you're a jewel,
Even in your present state.
You're a piece of coal under pressure,
But a diamond He'll create.

For the beauty to be revealed
Much pressing must be done,
Much time spent in His presence
Father God, Holy Spirit, Jesus Christ, the Son.

The only one, who can take our hearts, makes them all brand new.
See that lump of coal ... just wait till He gets through.

Oh, to be like Jesus, to shine with His love Divine.
He's creating in you a diamond
Oh, just look at you starting to shine.

Shine on with the love of Jesus
He is making all things new.
One of His most beautiful jewels
Is the diamond He's making out of you.

Just One Word

Just one word from the Master
Everything can change
Just one word from the Master
Your life He can rearrange.

Just one word from the Master
You can be made whole
Just one word from the Master
Can save your wounded soul.

There are also times He uses a process
There are times He takes some time
Either way the Father does it
That's up to Him, you're His design.

Still there are times He'll speak
And you'll know His voice you've heard.
You know your life is forever changed
Because Your Heavenly Father spoke one word.

Keep On Walking, My Faithful Friend

Keep on walking, my faithful friend,
Keep on walking till your journey's end.
Keep on walking with your Father God,
Many others a similar path have trod.

Keep on walking when you think you can't.
Keep on walking with each step He will grant.

Strength for your journey
Like you've never known
Blessed assurance
Of a victory won.

Keep on walking and don't you forget,
Father God is walking with you
And He's not finished with you yet.

When you feel like quitting
Like giving up.
Cling more tightly to Jesus
He'll lift you up.

Don't you listen
When the enemy is talking.
Just put one foot in front of the other and
KEEP ON WALKING!

Keep Pressing

Something I read several years ago came to my mind this morning that really helped me to complete those 5 miles!

My left knee was hurting pretty badly, causing me to limp along. Arthritis and what the doctor said was a Bakers cyst can be pretty painful at times.

I read that if you focus on something up ahead of you, it will help you while you walk.

So true! I prayed and continued to walk. I noticed though, that when I'd stop and pay attention to the pain it grew worse; *but*, when I found something to focus on out ahead of me, it was much easier, and I was able to complete my goal.

Here is what came to mind. "So we fix our eyes not on what is seen, for what is seen is temporary, but on what is unseen, for what is unseen is eternal." (*NKJV*, 2 Corinthians 4:18 paraphrased).

I noticed when I gave my attention to the pain, it seemed to grow worse. Now, did it all go away just because I didn't focus on it? No, it didn't. Yet, Father God gave me the ability to overcome and complete my goal.

Maybe today, you have a physical illness, or it may be a family crisis, or a financial hardship. Maybe today, you are simply overwhelmed by circumstances beyond your control.

Look up my friend; look unto Jesus Christ, the author and finisher of your faith! Look ahead in the distance, Jesus is coming soon and *all these trials* will soon be over. Look ahead to eternity spent with our beloved Savior, Jesus Christ!

Quit looking at your present circumstances. Simply do what Father God has told you to do in the circumstance and leave it to Him; and press on. "I press toward the goal for the prize of the upward call of God in Christ Jesus." (*NKJV*, Philippians 3:14). God bless and KEEP ON WALKING!

My Dearest Friend

Many a night, tormented and tossed,
Fearing for my life, that all was lost.
Then the Master rescued me,
Cleansed my soul and set me free.

Still there are times, I am afraid,
But for those times, His life He gave,
To save my soul and give me peace.
Only God provides this blessed reprieve.

No matter the storm, the pain within,
With Him I have a true and lasting friend.
He knows my every fault and sin
Still the God of all glory, time with me longs to spend.

It's amazing this love, I've finally found.
I could search the whole world over
None like His love could be found.

God's love is eternal, it will never end,
I'm so glad I finally found Him,
He is my dearest friend.

My Hope Is In You, Lord

My hope is in You, Lord,
In you alone.
Surrendered I kneel
Before your throne.

Your grace has found me
And set me free.
I'm no longer afraid
Of just being me.

Finally free
From the grip of fear,
Father. thank you
For drawing me near.

Thank you for forgiving me,
For lifting me up.
Thank you for loving me,
For cleansing my heart.

I'm still in that process
So much still to do
Yet this I know
You won't quit
Till You're through.

You are the potter,
I am the clay.
Mold me into your image
As I try Your will to obey.

Strengthen me Father,
I can't do it alone.
Surrendered, I kneel
Before Your throne.

No Greater Love

No greater love has ever been known,
Than when Father God chose to make us His own.
No one else would ever pay the price
No one else would lay down their life.

To redeem our sin-sick souls
Cleanse our hearts
Make us whole.

No one else would endure such shame
Already knowing we would deny His name.
He already knew the path we'd take
That at times we'd forsake Him,
And cause Him pain.

Still He chose to come, to die,
To pay the price for you and I.
He looked into the future you see,
There He saw you and me.

Living the life that He has planned
Free and forgiven
And learning to stand.

Learning to trust Him
To grow in God's grace.
One day, we'll see Him face to face.

We all have a part in God's grand design
To lead others to Jesus and our home on high.

Not Yet, Got a Little Pruning to Do!

Many times Father God's goodness is proven when He says, "Not yet." He doesn't send His children out unprepared. At times, we may want to get ahead of the process of preparation because yes, it's sometimes very painful and uncomfortable as He is molding and shaping us. Looking back over the last few years I'm starting to see how necessary, *so necessary*, the lessons have been in my life.

I'm so thankful that God loves us enough that He doesn't just quit when we get uncomfortable and let us have our own way like spoiled children. Father God continues to mold us and work things out in us to change us into His image, even while we're kicking and screaming! He is not going to quit just because I whine! He knows, in the end, the pain will pay off in the pruned person. The pruning will pay off in the ability to bear much fruit for Father God's kingdom, and peace and joy for the person He's pruning too!

Obedience

I woke up during the night with these thoughts on my mind. "For bodily exercise profits little: but godliness is profitable unto all things, having promise of the life that now is and of that which is to come." (*NKJV*, 1 Timothy 4:8).

As you all know, I have been talking about my walks; about how God speaks to me during these times and how much better I'm feeling and about losing weight. The real reason all this is helping me so much is wrapped up in one word, obedience!

Father God has dealt with me for a long time about walking in self-control and taking better care of myself, so that I will be able to do what He has given me to do. I won't lie, I enjoy looking better also, who doesn't?

I know that when we exercise, our bodies produce endorphins which give us what some call 'a runner's high' and I found this to be true. More than that though, it is simply because I know that this is one of many disciplines that God requires of us; to walk in self-control. "For the fruit of the

Spirit is love, joy, peace, long-suffering, kindness, goodness, faithfulness, gentleness and self-control." (*NKJV*, Galatians 5:22). Yes there it is self-control!

I must restrict certain things because I know the effect they have on me, and I know that I must add some things because I know the effect they have on me as well. For you, it may be in a different area that God has required more out of you. I don't know what your area may be but this I know, if you will take the step of obedience Father God will meet you there, and He will give you all you need to accomplish the task He has set before you!

Oh, Glorious Magnificent Thought

Oh glorious magnificent thought,
We have been bought.
Paid for
Ransomed from sin.

My chains are gone
No longer alone
I'm free from the grip of those chains.

Though I was to blame,
Still Jesus came.
My heart to heal and to save.

On Being Healed

A few days ago, I requested prayer from all of you, and last night I wrote about believing for *the impossible*. Today, before leaving church, two different people approached me and spoke to me that I had been healed! *I receive this word in Jesus' mighty name*! What the condition was is not really important except that it <u>was</u>, I repeat *was* a very serious, potentially life threatening virus that I had been living with for about 18 years, at least.

I had been experiencing some issues the last year or two, especially in the last few months, that were not good and really wasn't sure if they were related to the virus or not; because several conditions can have similar symptoms.

I had decided to and made an appointment with the gastroenterologist because this *was* a virus that affected my liver. I do plan to go ahead and see this doctor on November 12th. You know why? *I am believing to have tests done to confirm that Father God has already healed my liver, and all other effects the virus gave me when it was in my body!* You may call me crazy, say I'm going overboard. No matter, I have just decided, *yes, I have decided*, to take my Father, yes, My Father, *my heavenly Daddy, Abba and Father at His word*! I am writing this tonight in faith that I am *already healed*. Now I am believing to go get medical documentation to prove it and share it with the world in Jesus' name!

A few years ago I also had *major* problems with my feet; neuropathy, spurs, and plantar fasciitis. Yet, my Father God healed them! Wherever you are, whoever you are, don't give up! Your miracle may just be right around the corner! God Bless, and KEEP ON WALKING!

One Act of Obedience

There is absolutely *no situation*, not a single one that cannot be changed by the power of our Almighty Father God! Our human minds may not comprehend this; nevertheless, it's still true.

The Master, the Creator of the universe, Father God alone, has the power to do whatever He chooses. Whenever He chooses, and however He chooses!

Let's quit trying to figure out all the details, quit trying to *make* something happen. Let's choose to trust Him, and just do the next thing He has prompted us to do.

Many times things that we have been praying about for years begin to happen when we simply obey the smallest promptings of the Holy Spirit. Never discount that "seemingly small" thing that Father God has spoken to your heart to do. That one act of obedience may just lead to one of the biggest blessings in your life!

The Bible says, "But as it is written, eye has not seen, nor ear heard, neither have entered into the heart of man the things which God has prepared for them that love

Him." (*NKJV*, 1 Corinthians 2:9). What a promise! I can hardly wait to see what Father God will do next! God bless and KEEP ON WALKING!

One Right Decision

Don't give up! What if you're just one right decision away from your greatest blessing? Do you know that the Bible says in (*NKJV*, Isaiah 1:19), "If you are willing and obedient, you shall eat the good things of the land;" At times, it seems we're having many hard trials and things look bleak, but God is faithful always and performs His Word!

In (*NKJV*, Psalm 138:8), it says, "The Lord will perfect that *which* concerns me;" God is not a man, He cannot lie! He is going to take care of you and give you what you need. Hang on to His promises. The thing you've been praying for might just be closer than you realize. One thing is for certain, Father God is always right on time!

Only Trust Him

Take every thought captive
Make it obey.
Don't allow the devil's lies
To control your day.

You have the power
With God's Word it's true.
You can overcome those thoughts
That are trying to stop you.

Speak God's Word
Against Satan's lies.
Watch the enemy's schemes crumble
Before your very eyes.

We have the victory
It's already been won.
It's been paid for in full
By God's only begotten Son

Jesus paid in full
For everything we will ever need
Only trust Him, only believe

Only trust Him, and His Word obey
Give God your heart, why not today?
Why not today?
Tomorrow may be too late
Tomorrow's not promised
Please trust Him, don't wait.

Don't wait for a day
That may never come.
Today if you hear His voice, please listen, don't run.
Come to the Father, He's waiting for you.
With His love so amazing, He'll save and satisfy you.

Press Through the Pain

As I was walking this morning, a thought struck me about the second mile. The first one is painful, hurts the shins, the knees, especially if you're overweight, and yes I am. I've done this before and at times have lost about 80 pounds and felt great; and had so much more energy!

There really is a great burst of energy when you press through the pain and go the second mile! I started thinking; it's the same way spiritually. Discipline isn't easy! It isn't comfortable to get up early, or stay up late to spend time alone with God.

It isn't comfortable to be kind when you want to tell someone exactly what you think; when you want to cry but instead hide behind a smile. It isn't easy to do more than just what's required of you at times. Hold on though, your breakthrough may just be in the second mile! When we do what's right because we love God our Father and want to please Him, sure it may be painful, but hold on; your breakthrough, your peace and joy maybe just around the corner in the second mile.

"Whoever compels you to go one mile, go with him two." (*NKJV*, Matthew 5: 41).

Qualified

If you have ever felt the pain of being the last one chosen, maybe in school, remember how we used to "pick teams?" I ALWAYS hated that. I was usually last or very close to the last one chosen. I was never athletic, except for swimming and rollerskating! I loved Dollar Night at Funland Skate Castle! Remember skating the waltz, trucking or limbo? I was (still am) overweight; didn't have much money. I wasn't the popular one either. It is such an awful feeling, embarrassing to feel unwanted, for whatever reason. I, by no means, want sympathy, though I sure have wanted it at times.

Today my hubby and I were talking. He reminded me of King David. You know the little guy in the Bible who eventually became King? They didn't even bring him in from the field when they were looking for the one who would become King. Imagine that! They would have chosen one of his brothers over him for sure, the one that appeared more qualified. They, "the people," didn't even consider him! "They," would have never chosen him.

I am so thankful that Father God looks past all our weakness, our failures, our lack of discipline, our fear, and He still sees something; someone He can use for His glory! He still sees the gifts He placed inside of us from the very beginning. The point of this is to encourage you and myself. It does not matter where you came from, what your deficiencies/inabilities are. Father God can, and will use you and me to do whatever, *whatever, He decides*; not in our ability, not in our strength; *in His strength!* We however, do have to step up, step out, and be willing to try to do our part. What if David would have refused to be King simply because they didn't choose him first?

So what if we don't get picked on the first go round! We are chosen by God and what Father God has planned He will bring to pass! Sometimes many years of preparation are required to fulfill Father God's plan for us. You see, no matter what, Father God doesn't just give up on us and let us quit. He doesn't forsake us. If Father God has special work for you to do, He has not forgotten it. He will keep calling us to come forward and fulfill what He's placed in our heart. God bless and KEEP ON WALKING!!

Quit Rehearsing!

Have you ever had a particular thought or future event consume your thought process? Not just bad things, but maybe a good thing too? Something you think could happen, and you spend lots of "now time" rehearsing it in your mind. I realized this morning I have been doing exactly that; spending lots of time thinking about something that may or may not happen; not a bad thing, just a thing. I'm reminded of this scripture. "Therefore do not worry about tomorrow, for tomorrow will worry about its own things." (*NKJV*, Matthew 6:34). Does this mean we make no plans? Of course not! Just don't worry. We should do our best to make wise decisions and leave the rest to Father God.

In (*NKJV*, 2 Corinthians 10:5), it says, "casting down arguments and every high thing that exalts itself against the knowledge of God." Sometimes, they may not be bad things, just things that are trying to take our focus off of today; to take our energy away from what we need to be focusing on at this point in our lives.

God has been blessing me so wonderfully these past few weeks, some I've shared with you, some I haven't. I realized again today, I just need to focus on the thing He is doing right now and not use today's energy on tomorrow's events! God goes before us to prepare the way. He's got it! I've decided to leave the future events to Him; just take the next step, while I enjoy today! How about you? God bless and KEEP ON WALKING!

Remember The Lemon Drops!

This morning as I was doing my Bible study, a particular line stood out to me. "What seems like a drop in the bucket to you may be a wellspring of life to someone else!" This is so true. I can still remember a little older lady from my childhood, Mrs. Hargett was her name. She would drive around in her little car in the low-income housing where we lived at the time, and she would pass out lemon drops and invite us to Vacation Bible School.

This little lady came all by herself, she wasn't afraid; or if she was, she did it anyway. I was raised in church. I have a precious Christian Momma, so I already knew about Jesus. I still welcomed our visits in the neighborhood from Mrs. Hargett. She was such a sweet lady. She obviously had an impact on my life. I still remember her thirty-five years later!

I wonder what kind of impact she had on those children who didn't have anyone to show them the love of Jesus? What if her simple act of kindness was the only kind act some of those children ever saw? What would this one act of kindness mean to a child who didn't have a Christian Mother or Dad? What would it have meant to a child who had never heard of Jesus?

I remember this one act of kindness, thirty-five years later. I am simply saying if Father God prompts you to do something, by all means, *do it*! No act of kindness goes unnoticed by our Father God. We may never know this side of eternity how one seemingly small thing changed a person's life forever. One simple thing that we may take for granted. A drop in the bucket to us because we are accustomed to being blessed. This one drop may be a wellspring of life to those who are in need.

Never take for granted those simple promptings from the Lord. He may tell you to cook someone a meal, wash their car, pray with them, tell them they look pretty today, that you are proud of them, etc. Never underestimate the power and lasting influence of one, *just one* seemingly small act of kindness. Rest assured Father God takes notice. KEEP ON WALKING!

Seemingly Silent

While walking this morning I was wondering what the Lord might speak to my heart today. You know what? It seemed He was silent today. I continued to walk, praying some but mostly just walking. The thought came to me, that's really how life is. Sometimes we hear with clarity, sometimes we can barely hear Him whisper, if we can hear Him at all.

Father God is always speaking through His Word. He may not always give us those 'thunderbolt and lightning' experiences we would like, yet He still speaks. He may give us direction in many different ways, through His Word, through a friend, in quiet times of fasting and prayer. He may simply speak to us in that still, small voice that brings such peace.

Father God is always faithful to guide His children, rest assured. One thing I know for sure is this: He alone knows exactly what we need to know, and when we need to know it. He will guide us as we begin to step out in faith as He has told us to do. What He had planned for us from the beginning, He still has planned for us today. What if I mess up and take a wrong step? What if I blow it?

Don't you think that He already knew every mistake, every choice, we would ever make before He blew His breath into us? Yes, of course, He already knew. In (*NKJV*, Jeremiah 1:5), it says, "Before I formed you in the womb I knew you." Wow! He chose us, handpicked us for His service. Think about that!

Rest in the fact that the very one who gives you your breath, knows every detail of your life; nothing takes Him by surprise! Next time you're having a little trouble hearing Him just keep doing the last thing He told you to do, until He gives you the next step. Put one foot in front of the other and KEEP ON WALKING!

Settling in Silence

"Unless the Lord had been my help, My soul would soon have settled in silence. If I say, 'My foot slips,' Your mercy, O Lord, will hold me up. In the multitude of my anxieties within me, Your comforts delight my soul." (*NKJV*, Psalm 94: 17-19).

I understand this because I was close to death when Father God rescued me. It also speaks to me that unless God had rescued me from my fear and insecurity and lack of purpose, I too, would have just kept settling for the same old things I've always done; just because it's comfortable or because it's all I knew to do. I would have settled for things the way they've always been; good but maybe not to my full potential. I would have settled in silence. No more!

The Lord has held me up, healed me and given me a dream, a purpose to pursue. Oh, the joy of purpose, a vision! The Word of God says, "without a vision my people perish." You see God created us for a reason; we are not here by happenstance. (*NKJV*, Jeremiah 29:11), says that "God knows the plans He has for us, to prosper us and not to harm us, to give us a hope and a future."

So today, let's choose to cast off everything that would hinder God's plan for our life. Let's choose to be a God chaser and pursue the dream He has placed inside our heart. I'm sure you have a dream. You may not have discovered it yet, but it's in there. You may have already discovered it and have let fear or people's opinion stop you. Today, let's remember, if God is for us who can be against us? If the God of heaven chose you, my sister or brother, you ain't got nothing to fear! Come on, let's get going! Our destiny is waiting! God bless and KEEP ON WALKING!

Sometimes I Get Sideways

Sometimes I get sideways
Twisted around
Straying from the path
I finally found.

I lose my direction
My vision gets blurred.
I find it hard
To remember Your words.

The promises you've given
Yes, sometimes I doubt.
I wonder, will I make it?
Will I ever get out?

Free from *all* bondage
I long to be.
To run with freedom
This race set for me.

Then my Father speaks gently,
"Come closer to me.
I alone can take you
Where you long to be."

Keep On Walking

Quit trying to forge the path
On your own.
Listen more closely
My will shall be shown.

In quietness, wait
On the proper time.
In my plan, you'll flourish
Not your will, but Mine.

My plan is best
For I have known from the start
Just what you need
For I created your heart.

Yes, through each twist and turn,
Every lesson learned,
I've been here waiting
For you to return.

I've not thrown away
My plans for you.
Come with me, My child
I've been waiting for you.

Spectacular Grace

Every once in a while
I take a look back
At the pain and destruction
That are part of my past.

God allows me to see
How far we've come.
The joy in my life
All the victories now won.

You see, our past is just a reminder
Of the spectacular grace of God
Of all the times He rescued us
And saved us from great harm.

I'm so humbled at this knowing
That my King Jesus died for me.
For I know without His sacrifice
I never would have been set free.

Tell Me

Tell me your stories of days gone by,
Of how God's been faithful
Your tears to dry.

Tell me your stories of days long ago,
How Father God made things happen
When the whole world said no.

Tell me of His faithfulness all of your days,
His kindness, His goodness, His marvelous ways.

Tell me of your struggles, your pain and fears,
Yet that God was still faithful all through the years.

Cause sometimes we need someone who's been there,
To know they understand; to know that they care.

That even when I'm weak, His arms are opened wide.
His love will never change
He is forever mine.

Thankful

I am thankful for ice cubes and ketchup! Yes, there is a story behind this statement. About 18 years ago, I was living at a place called Restoration Ranch. This was the place Father God used to help me when He set me free from alcohol addiction, among many other things. The Ranch, as I'll call it, was run at that time solely on donations, needless to say, things were limited.

We ate what was donated; all our utilities were paid with donations, etc. I recall two of the things I really missed having were (believe it or not) ice cubes and ketchup! Why we didn't have some of those old fashioned ice trays, I don't remember. We may have had them and the ones working in the kitchen just didn't bother to fill them, I don't know. My problem was that I wasn't getting ice cubes like I wanted! You know us southerners love some ice tea; with lemon for me thank you!

Having no ketchup was also an issue for me. I even dip potato chips in ketchup sometimes. We didn't have much ketchup either, if any. You may be asking why is she even talking about this? I was approached here recently at church, and asked what are some of the reasons I am thankful? We are putting together a video for thanksgiving.

Jesus, of course, is on the top of the list; my family, my church, my job, and there are so many more very serious things I could talk about. I've come to realize also that we need to pay attention to *all* the reasons we have to be thankful. There are so many things that Father God blesses us with that we can just take for granted if we don't *decide on purpose* to be thankful. Sometimes we need to just take a look around us and see just how many reasons we *truly do have* to be thankful. Yes, today among many, many other things, I am still thankful for ice cubes and ketchup! KEEP ON WALKING!

That Resurrection Morning

Mercy in abundance
Rich and free,
Grace to pardon our sin
Available for you and me.

The devil tried to stop it
To thwart God's plan.
To keep us from receiving
Salvation from God's hand.

That Resurrection morning
When Jesus Christ arose,
The devil was defeated
You can rest assured he knows.

That forever it is finished
The debt we owed was paid,
Sin and death no longer win,
For King Jesus has conquered the grave!

The Champion Steps In

Right in the middle of your darkest night;
Right in the center of your hardest fight;
Right when you thought you'd never get back up,
Right when you thought you weren't strong enough,

Into your fight steps your Champion;
Your warrior, your Savior, your very best Friend;
Into your fight steps your soon-coming King.
There's no way you can lose with Him in the ring.

Just in time your Champion steps in.
The victory is yours, just cling to Him.
Yes the battle is fierce, that's for sure.
You can't be defeated with Almighty God in your corner.

The Gift Inside

Have you tried to be someone that you're really not?
Have you tried many times to fill the wrong spot?
Have you looked to other's opinions to see if you're okay?
My friend that's not necessary.
There is a better way.

The One who created you, calls you by name;
Designed you as He desired. Never be ashamed.
The Master Himself handcrafted you,
Maybe some bad choices have dulled your view.

Maybe some wrong choices have caused some harm.
It's not too late, don't be alarmed.
You see, the Master Craftsman knows His design,
He knows exactly what it takes to get you in line.

He knows the reason He created you
If you keep on searching, you'll find the right door.
When you walk through it, you'll know this is it.
You finally found your purpose,
You've now unwrapped your gift.

The River of God

The river of God is deep and wide,
In the river of God is where I long to abide.
It's refreshing to my spirit and gives me life.
In this river there's no sorrow or strife.

The river is running, won't you jump in?
There the Father is waiting to cleanse you from sin.

The river is powerful.
It can't be stopped.
It flows from heaven,
Straight from our God.

Everyone is invited, not a person left out.
That in itself makes me want to shout.

So, here's your invitation,
Won't you please come in?
You will not be disappointed,
As your new life begins.

Joy and freedom like you've never known,
Just jump on in
And let your heart become God's home.

This World Ain't Always Sunshine and Roses

"This world ain't always sunshine and roses! It isn't about how hard you hit. It's how many hits you can take and still keep moving forward." Wow! I've heard this line spoken by many people in my life. Not really what you expect to hear Father God speak, right? Yet speak, He did!

I went for a walk this morning and to be honest, I was feeling kind of overwhelmed with everything. This is what I told the Lord in so many words, "Yes Lord, I'll keep walking though I may not understand; though I can't figure it all out." I don't have to. No, I don't know how it will all work out. I don't have to, because You know and You are faithful.

I'm usually one of my worst critics. If I don't feel I'm doing good enough, or being the best example of God's peace and strength, I tend to beat myself up. Is anyone else out there like this? I know there is, which is probably why I'm writing this. I tend to get aggravated when I don't feel like I have enough strength. Then, just when Father

God knows I'm at my strengths end, He lovingly steps in, and simply asks, "Won't you let Me help you? I alone can carry you through whatever hardship this life may bring. I alone *am* your strength. I alone give you the ability to keep moving forward." "My grace is sufficient for you, for my strength is made perfect in weakness." (*NKJV*, 2 Corinthians 12:9).

I guess the point of this is simply this. We don't have to do this alone. We don't have to try to be strong enough to handle everything. We simply cannot, but Father God can! His strength is made perfect in our weakness.

So today, if you're running low on strength, or maybe you don't feel that peace and joy; just run quickly to the Master, Father God! Don't hesitate! He alone has the endless supply of all we will ever need! God bless and yes, KEEP ON WALKING!

Though I May Not Understand How This Can Be Part of Your Plan

Though I may not understand how this can
be part of your plan,
You've proven Yourself faithful
Time and time again.

I trust you, Father,
Please help me stand,
Amidst uncertain times at hand.

My flesh is weak and crying out,
My heart is breaking as I shout.
Please help my spirit to receive
Peace and rest, your blessed reprieve.

I know our times are in Your hands,
In Your strength Lord, help me stand.
All glory to You Lord, to You alone,
As I wait before your throne.

For clear direction
I know You'll give,
As my life for You I live.

Tomorrow Is Not Promised

He sees you there,
With your head hung low.
He sees your heart,
Broken and torn.

He longs to save you,
And set you free.
He gave His life for your ransom, you see.

You don't have to live in fear and shame.
It was for you that our Savior came.
Come to the cross and give Him your all,
Please listen today to the Father's call.

Tomorrow is not promised.
Today is the day.
The Savior is calling,
Please listen, don't wait.

There's no greater joy
than obeying His voice
But it's up to you.
He gave you the choice.
He's calling you.
Please answer His call,
It was for you that He gave His all.

Wham!

Do you ever notice that when you begin to make progress in a certain area, you are immediately met with resistance, fear and maybe even confusion? You may be daring to dream the impossible when all of a sudden it hits you *wham*! Me too. This however, is not supposed to stop us! (*NKJV*, 1 Peter 5:8), says, "Be sober, be vigilant, because your adversary the devil walks about like a roaring lion." Take note, *like a roaring lion*!

You see, the devil can only devour us *if we let him*. If you're a Christian, the Almighty God, the One and only true and living God, lives inside of you! There is no way the enemy can defeat you, unless you quit; unless you give up. (*NKJV*, Isaiah 54:17), says, "No weapon formed against you shall prosper, and every tongue *which* rises, against you in judgment You shall condemn."

These aren't my words, these are the words of the Master! The reason the enemy is fighting you so hard is he knows, *rest assured he knows*, if we, God's children, ever fully realize how much He loves us and that we really can do the impossible through Christ. Satan won't be able to keep using the same old tricks against us.

Today, let's choose to pick up weapons, let's begin to take Father God at His Word and move forward into all that, He has planned for us. Let's not take for granted the freedom that Father God has granted us. Refuse to let the enemy steal from you any longer! Pick your heads up, saints! We have got work to do, and Father God's love to share! KEEP ON WALKING!

What About Those Spots?

Have you ever been doing something totally ordinary and have Father God speak to you about a spiritual situation? I just got back from walking, and started to fix the hubby some supper. I am peeling red potatoes; you know the kind that can have little spots on them that we ladies like to peel off. This one in particular had lots of dark places and knots. I thought to myself, *"by the time I get through trimming this one, there won't be much left. There is still some good left though, so I won't throw it away."*

There it is. You may feel like you have so many dark places, spots, sins, insecurities and failings that Father God can't or worse yet, won't use you. This my, friend, is simply *not true*! The Bible says in (*NKJV*, 2 Corinthians 12:9 paraphrased), that "God's grace is sufficient for us, that His strength is made perfect in our weakness,." You see, He knew all about these "spots," these shortcomings, these sins before we were ever even born; and still, He chose us!

Father God desires to use us for His glory. He wants to have a personal relationship with us. Isn't this amazing? You see, He also knows the good stuff He has placed inside each one of us. He knows what gifts and abilities He has placed inside each one of us. He alone knows exactly how and when to trim those "dark spots"" off, without ruining the "potato" (the gift inside). He knows just how to peel His potatoes (us, His kids.). Isn't that something? KEEP ON WALKING!

What Would You Do?

What would you do
If you dared to dream;
Instead of living your life
From behind the scenes?

What would you do
If there were no limits;
If you chose to believe
You really could live it?

The life that you've dreamed about
But never, never told.
The vision inside you,
you long to take hold.

It's God given,
You know it.
No matter what they say,
Never let them stop your voice
Just listen and obey.

Speak only what I tell you.
Don't let your focus stray,
Just calmly walk beside Me.
Trust me and obey.

Don't Get Over It, Get Rid of It!

When you tell someone to "get over it," make sure you understand what that means. The only way to solve something is to get rid of it, or at least try to understand it. The same way a man may say, "Get over it," but yet if he's ever hurt emotionally, they say he withdraws into a cave. You don't get another chance. A woman can also 'get over it' usually resulting in lack of sex or closeness because she is dealing with getting over it by protecting her emotions. Don't expect intimacy of any sort if you always tell each other to "get over it." You must work to *get through it*, and at least be willing to compromise in love. (*NKJV*, Romans 12:10), says, "Be devoted to one another in love. Honor one another above yourselves."

Who Makes Me Thankful

This is my official day number three of what, or actually, who makes me thankful. I am thankful for my wonderful Momma. Without her, I don't know what would have happened to me. She stood by me through all my years of rebellion and addiction to alcohol. She loved me unconditionally. She never gave up on me. I am sure it would have been easy to give up, had she only looked at the circumstances. I am so glad she didn't give up. Instead, she looked to Father God, and He answered her prayers for her little girl to be saved and to be delivered.

There were lots of others also praying for me, I know. My Momma was always there right beside me, loving me, and showing me Jesus, through her life. I learned to trust Him because of her. If she were reading this, she would probably say something like this, "I'm not perfect, I've made a lot of mistakes." That's the beauty of it! She taught me that even though we do sin, we mess up; we don't always get it right; *we can be forgiven*!

We can simply begin again by being sorry for our sins, and asking Father God to forgive us. She made it easy to understand. Even when I was a drunken sinner, Father God still loved me. He still wanted me. She taught me about Father God's amazing love, His marvelous grace.

At times, I may get a little too personal for some of you; maybe some of you aren't comfortable with the details of your past. I am not happy about mine either. The magnificent thing is we have a personal God, who knows every single, sordid, humiliating, thing we've ever done. You know what? He will always love us just the same. That's wonderful news! I am so thankful that I have a precious Momma who taught me the really important things. KEEP ON WALKING!

Why Not Me?

Whosoever will dream?
Dare to take a chance
Quit living their lives
Through happenstance

Whosoever believes God's Word is true,
Nothing is impossible; it's up to you.
Will you go on living, as you always have?
Or will you trust Him and take that chance?

Will you surrender to the plans God has,
Or simply exist, and forever be scared?
Letting fear rule you
Instead of trusting God.

Trust in the vision
God has placed in your hands.
He is well able to bring it to pass.

Yet fight you must to realize your dreams,
Don't fall prey to the enemy's schemes.

Discouragement, fear, insecurity too
Are, part of the enemy's plan.

He's trying to stop you.
Don't let him win, keep moving forward.
Father God will guide you
As you journey onward.

All things are possible
With Father God you see,
Just dare to believe
Why not me?

You Are Mine

A scared little girl from long ago,
Sometimes lingers here inside my soul.
She questions things the way they are.
Sometimes she runs but never far.

She holds onto me,
In fear of her life,
Afraid to let go,
And see the look in their eyes.

What should I say?
I wonder will they push me; away?
Am I good enough?
Will they love me?
Oh how I long to just be me.

Then Father God whispers,
"It's ok to be you,
Little girl, or grown woman.
I created the two."

You are mine; you're unique;
You're gifted and Divine
You only need My light to shine

Shine on my daughter,
With the gifts I have given.
It's for my glory,
To this place you are driven.

Never let anything
Hinder your dream.
Come with me my daughter,
Simply dare to trust Me.

You Have a Purpose

We're all created to be a part,
We're God's creation, His work of art.
Each one designed for a specific task,
Do I really matter?
I'm glad you asked.

The part that's missing may just be you.
No one else can fulfill what you're created to do.
You have a purpose, planned by God
To make a difference, to change your world.

We were created to be part of a whole,
To give and receive, to work towards a common goal.
To bring others to Christ,
To share His love abroad,
To simply be a part
Of the family of God.

Author Bio

My name is Jeana Willis. I am 48 years old. I was born in Port Sulphur, Louisiana. I was raised by my precious, Godly Momma, Verna Pitts Neville. I have been married to a wonderful Christian man, Jerry Willis, for 17 years. We have no children, just two spoiled cats, Emily and Esther.

I accepted the Lord Jesus as my Savior at a very young age, but in my teenage years, I went far in the opposite direction and ended up spending several years in a life of addiction, desperation and turmoil. Yet, through all my rebellion, Father God still loved me and called me back to Himself. I would like to say I came back easily, but it was a long, hard road. I received four DUIs, served time in jail, and partook in the sin that goes with that lifestyle. I ended up on what could have been my deathbed.

BUT GOD! He so mercifully rescued me and set me free from alcohol and all kinds of sin! The day when I gave my heart back to Him, I was lying in bed, after almost drinking myself to death. I prayed, "Lord, if

You will get me out of this, I don't know what I will do or how, but I will not come back here again."

My friend, Father God heard my desperate cry that day and rescued me. I have been living for Him since that day about 20 years ago. No matter who, you are, or how far you may have fallen my friend, *there is hope in Father God*!

"He sent from above, He took me. He drew me out of many waters. He delivered me from my strong enemy, and from those who hated me, for they were too strong for me. They confronted me in the day of my calamity, but the Lord was my support. He brought me out into a broad place; He delivered me because He delighted in me." (*NKJV*, Psalm 18:16-19).

www.ingramcontent.com/pod-product-compliance
Lightning Source LLC
Chambersburg PA
CBHW051838090426
42736CB00011B/1871